COMPANIES DON'T SUCCEED, PEOPLE DO

50 Ways to MOTIVATE Your Team

Bob Nelson PhD

Bestselling Author of *1501 Ways to Reward Employees*

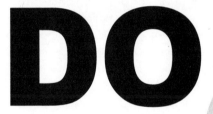

simple truths
small books. BIG IMPACT.

Photo Credits
Internals: pages 7, 13, 22, 97, phipatbig/Shutterstock; page 16, Sudjino/iStock; page 19, danielfela/Shutterstock; pages 24–25 Leremy/Shutterstock; page 30, america365/Shutterstock; page 33, VasRomanovya Kobelev/Shutterstock; page 39, Askold Romanov/Shutterstock; page 43, OlgaSha/Shutterstock; page 46, gst/Shutterstock; page 54, Vectorstock; page 60, Vectorstock; page 63, Dragana Gerasimoski/Shutterstock; page 68–69, alex.makarova/Shutterstock; page 75, phipatbig/Shutterstock; page 79, Josep.Ng/Shutterstock; page 88, Arcady/Shutterstock; page 91, VectorStock; page 94, Leremy/Shutterstock

Published by Simple Truths, an imprint of Sourcebooks, Inc.
P.O. Box 4410, Naperville, Illinois 60567-4410
(630) 961-3900
Fax: (630) 961-2168
www.sourcebooks.com

Printed and bound in the United States of America.
WOZ 10 9 8 7 6 5 4 3 2 1

IF YOU WANT TO GO FAST, GO ALONE. IF YOU WANT TO GO FAR, GO TOGETHER.

—AFRICAN PROVERB

Introduction

Even the most talented individual soon realizes that the secret to achieving more in business and in life is through mastering the art of motivating others. No one is an island; we are each dependent upon others throughout our lives to get things done that are important to us. In fact, my former professor, the late, great Peter Drucker, defined management as "getting things done through others."

As obvious as this sounds, motivating a team of divergent individuals, each of whom has different talents, personalities, goals, and ambitions, is much easier said than done. This is why *Companies Don't Succeed, People Do* is so valuable for you. In it, you will find real stories, techniques, and examples from successful leaders who have all tried to do the same thing: increase the motivation, performance, and success of their teams.

Reflect on their advice and successes, and try what has worked. If you could do two things to make your teams more effective, what would they be? Or, better yet, share this information with members of your team, and challenge them to think of ways all of you can enhance your team performance. Use the ideas in this book as a starting point for discussion about improving your teams, achieving more, and being more successful.

Best of success,

Bob Nelson

NO ONE IS AN ISLAND;

we are each dependent upon others throughout

our lives to get things done that are important to us.

SUCCESS
INNOVATION
PRODUCTIVITY

Hire the Right People

"The secret of my success is that we have gone to exceptional lengths to hire the best people in the world."

—Steve Jobs

Holy Cross Hospital in Chicago uses a multifaceted approach to hiring new employees. Applicants are interviewed by teams of employees, including potential coworkers, department leaders, and human resources staff. Candidates are then divided into teams of four to eight people, and they are asked to take on a joint problem-solving exercise. The highest-rated applicants are then hired.

Continuously Share Your Vision

"To succeed in business it is necessary to make others see things as you see them."

—*John H. Patterson*

It's been said that the three keys to purchasing real estate are location, location, location. Here are the three keys to inspiring change: reinforce, reinforce, reinforce. In times of change, many leaders grossly underestimate the need for continuous reinforcement. Once the management team has signed off on the change message, the challenge is to keep it alive until behavior is consistent with your goals. It won't happen on its own. You need to have a plan in place to make it happen.

Answering these three questions is the first step for success:

1. How do I keep it simple? Less is always more.
2. How can I make it memorable?
3. How many times can I communicate it on a daily, weekly, and monthly basis?

To some this may sound like simple, commonsense stuff. But to do it right, it's anything but simple. It takes creative planning and input from everyone involved. But, most of all, it takes tremendous discipline to keep the train on the track. A lot of little things will make a big difference in convincing the team you're 100 percent committed to making change happen. So sweat the small stuff and remember: reinforce, reinforce, reinforce.

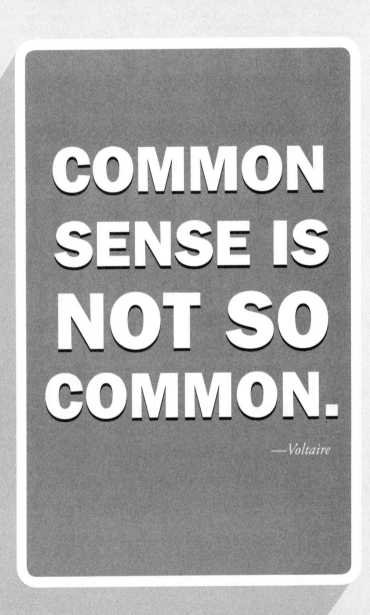

COMMON SENSE IS NOT SO COMMON.

—*Voltaire*

Learn to Communicate Effectively

"Communication works for those who work at it."

—*John Powell*

Contribute your ideas early and often in a team discussion. According to research presented in a book I wrote with Roger K. Mosvick called *We've Got to Start Meeting Like This!: A Guide to Successful Meeting Management*, when an individual engages in a team discussion within the first five minutes, that person is more likely to have greater influence in the meeting. When you wait fifteen or twenty minutes before making your first contribution, you will have much less influence on the discussion (about half as much as the early speaker). If you wait to speak until the middle of the meeting, your contributions will usually be ignored and have virtually no influence on the team's decision. Make an effort to contribute early in the discussion, even if it is only to ask a question or clarify a comment, to show that you are an active part of the discussion.

Set the Stage with New Hires

"Team player: one who unites others toward a shared destiny through sharing information and ideas, empowering others, and developing trust."

—Dennis Kinlaw

IT consulting firm Akili Inc., based in Irving, Texas, involves employees right from the start. In their orientation program, new recruits are issued mock passports and must acquire at least twenty stamps from fellow workers. New employees receive the stamps for attending a company event, recounting company folklore, or drawing the organizational chart correctly. This unique orientation process helps people become steeped in company values and culture quickly.

Catapult Systems, headquartered in Austin, Texas, has a "boot camp" program for new hires led by Chairman Sam Goodner to immerse them in the company culture before they take on any tasks. The topics include the roles of different departments in the company, customer service policies, and job responsibilities. New hires are given pop quizzes to check their retention of names and job titles of people they've met.

An Attitude of Ownership

"Never tell people how to do things. Tell them what to do and they will surprise you with their ingenuity."

—*George S. Patton*

To create an environment that embraces entrepreneurial thinking, consider these three keys:

ONE: Explain the company's mission, its goals, and most importantly, its strategies to achieve these goals. If employees understand the big picture, they are much more likely to understand their roles and why the company values their contributions.

TWO: Help your employees understand the competition. Appealing to their competitive nature and their pride can generate excellent results.

THREE: Encourage risk-taking and innovative thinking. Great leaders know that long-term survival depends on taking risks.

Collaborate
for Success

"Becoming skilled at doing more with others may be the single most important thing you can do to increase your value—regardless of your level of authority."

—*Christopher Avery*

Ubuntu is a South African tradition of unity and collaboration made famous by Nelson Mandela when he used it to unify the country after the fall of apartheid. *Ubuntu!* is also the title of a book this author wrote with Dr. Stephen Lundin about this powerful topic. In essence, the philosophy is "I am because we are" and stresses the importance of beginning together with a unified perspective in order to overcome challenges and obstacles.

The accounting department at Rady Children's Hospital in San Diego, California, has brought this powerful African tradition into their workplace. They've declared every Thursday "Ubuntu Day." All employees wear dashikis, a traditional colorful African shirt, as a public reminder of their unified desire to collaborate together. On Ubuntu Days, employees are encouraged to suggest ideas for their departments to function better, such as process improvements, cost-saving ideas, and innovations. They meet to discuss the ideas and to help each other implement the best ones.

Use Creativity to Think Outside the Box

"The most important thing I learned from big companies is that creativity gets stifled when everyone's got to follow the rules."

—*David Kelley*

Communicate the goal, then let the team figure out how to get there. When Carmen Villarma, president of The Management Group, a property management firm based in Vancouver, Washington, and Portland, Oregon, needed to rent out a new 416-unit apartment complex in a hurry, she approached a group of millennial employees at the company with a challenge. "Here are the keys to the office," she said. "You can work whenever you want; you can do whatever you need to in order to get this apartment complex rented."

The team of young workers rose to the occasion, making several YouTube videos, launching a Twitter campaign, and hosting parties for open houses. They succeeded in getting all units in the complex rented in record time. The group received sales commission for their work and decided to celebrate their success with a group trip to Las Vegas. Although one of the team members didn't meet her goal on the project, the group wanted her to come to Las Vegas with them because she had supported other team members along the way. When they returned from the trip, the group was ready for the next challenge, asking Carmen, "Do you have any other apartment complexes you need rented out?"

LAS VEGAS

Keep Your Employees Engaged

"We have to get everybody in the organization involved. If you do that right, the best ideas will rise to the top."

—*Jack Welch*

Harness the energy, ambition, and talent of your team members or risk losing them. Donna Wells, vice president of sales at Shutters Wholesale in Alpharetta, Georgia, shared an example of a millennial employee who said she was planning to leave the company because she had exhausted the available growth opportunities. Donna challenged the employee to come up with a plan outlining what she could achieve if supported by company management. The employee followed through, setting up an aggressive yearly sales plan that took the company into new markets and then successfully achieved those goals within just four months.

Once a quarter, Facebook has a Hack Day. (Hack is a positive term that means someone who can figure things out—a very successful programmer.) On Hack Day, every employee, no matter what his or her job, can work on something of his or her own choice to make Facebook a better place, helping to serve and deliver value to customers. Stuart Crabb, global director of learning, said he wished he could bring everyone in to experience Hack Day. "We have a group of very committed people already, but they explode with excitement on Hack Day with the fun of pursuing their own ideas. This empowers employees to feel there are no limits and can take on the world," said Crabb.

COMPANIES DON'T SUCCEED, PEOPLE DO!

During one of their Hack Days, employees conceived Facebook's legendary "Like" button, which is now a major part of the Facebook brand.

See Your Organization Through the Eyes of a Coworker

"Could a greater miracle take place than
for us to look through each other's
eyes for an instant?"

—*Henry David Thoreau*

Disney's theme parks close twice a year so all employees, called "cast members," can bring their families to enjoy the parks as guests while management runs the rides, serves the concessions, and wears the costumes, demonstrating that everyone is on the same team.

COMPANIES DON'T SUCCEED, PEOPLE DO!

At Mary Kay, Inc., all office staff exchange places with manufacturing employees once a year for a day of learning and empathy they call Spring Fling. When employees understand how different areas of the company work, they are more apt to make decisions that benefit the company as a whole, rather than solely benefiting their own department or group. Give your employees the opportunity to learn other people's jobs. Some organizations go as far as switching employee roles on a daily, weekly, or monthly basis. At pawn broker Cash America International, Inc., all employees from the receptionist to the CEO work four hours a week in one of their pawn shops.

Don't forget your managers. Have top executives spend a few days working on the front lines with customers or directly with your product. They'll have a new appreciation for what employees go through on the job. Hyatt Hotels Corp. has its executives visit properties multiple times a year, where they help check in guests, carry their bags, and help local staff members with their jobs.

Encourage Diversity

"Strength lies in differences, not in similarities."

—*Stephen R. Covey*

A group of Googlers organized an event called the Sum of Google at their headquarters in Mountain View, California. Designed to celebrate their culture of diversity with food, music, dance performances, and executive speakers, the Sum of Google has since grown and now lasts the entire month of July. Recently, more than five thousand Googlers in seventy offices across Asia, Europe, Latin America, and North America were engaged in global diversity and inclusion conversations through panel discussions and speakers.

Consider the global design and innovation consulting firm Continuum, which hires a diverse array of traditional designers, engineers, psychologists, artists, MBAs, and ethnographers. This pool of talent assembles as needed around client projects, sometimes working on several projects at a time. Continuum is deliberate about securing clients from a variety of fields so employees are exposed to a diverse set of design and business challenges and can share ideas from different industries, life experiences, and cultural perspectives.

DIVERSITY:
the art of thinking

ndependently
ogether.

—Malcolm Forbes

Keep Everything Transparent

"I motivate players through communication, being honest with them, having them respect and appreciate your ability and your help."

—*Tommy Lasorda*

Marketing software company HubSpot in Cambridge, Massachusetts, believes in transparency and revealing everything to its employees—from cash burn rates to comments on their wiki page. Founder and CEO Brian Halligan said that this transparency is just one aspect of their push toward a corporate culture of teamwork and collaboration. Halligan believes that the millennial generation has radically changed the way employees work and live and that companies need to change the way they manage. HubSpot works to create an extremely flat, transparent organization to meet the expectations of its employees.

Halligan doesn't have an office, and his salary is not that different from other employees. HubSpot employees have no problem calling him out on the firm's wiki page. Halligan believes that employees today have grown up with social media and expect transparency and authenticity from their leaders.

Failing Forward

> "You can tell a lot about the long-term viability of any organization simply by looking at how they handle mistakes."
>
> —*Bill Gates*

At the Hershey Company in Hershey, Pennsylvania, the late former chairman and CEO Richard Zimmerman wanted to encourage employees to exercise initiative in their jobs and take risks without fear of retribution. To encourage such risks, the Exalted Order of the Extended Neck Award was created. According to Zimmerman, "We wanted to reward people who were willing to buck the system, practice a little entrepreneurship, who were willing to stand the heat for an idea they really believe in." The award was given out on numerous occasions, including to a maintenance worker who devised a way to perform midweek cleaning on a piece of machinery without losing running time. Similarly, Google attributes much of its incredible success to failure. Like Zimmerman, Google's management team of Eric Schmidt, Larry Page, and Sergey Brin have explicitly stated the importance of "failing forward."

Remove Barriers

"When you're up to your rear end in alligators, it's hard to remember that your purpose is draining the swamp."

—George Napper

Job number one for any leader in times of change is to start removing the barriers that will keep your team from executing the plan. For example, if the plan calls for creating a customer first culture, you must identify any obstacles or barriers that will prevent you from achieving your goal. These obstacles usually fall into one of four categories:

ONE: Outdated systems
TWO: Outdated procedures

THREE: Outdated people

FOUR: A combination thereof

The first and most important part of this challenge is to do some serious diligence to clearly define the "enemy." This requires getting input from everyone, especially those frontline employees who are dealing directly with the customers. Your answers will come if you listen carefully to what they have to say. However, fixing what's broken will take longer, especially if the finger is pointed at outdated systems. Fixing problems caused by outdated procedures and outdated people can take less time but are just as critical to the change process.

Obstacles to change vary greatly; they can be 20,000–pound boulders or many small trees. Your job as a leader is to start cutting the trees as quickly as you can so your employees become convinced that good things are about to happen.

Self-Managed Teams

"Teamwork is the secret that makes common people achieve uncommon results."

—*Ifeanyi Enoch Onuoha*

Workers become empowered when they are trusted with the responsibility to carry out tasks that are normally within the province of management. The implementation of self-directed work teams at Florida's Aero Technical Components has freed workers to make decisions formerly made by management. The result: lower costs and better products. "Before you had to go to somebody and ask what you had to do all the time, and now you put out a better product," said machine operator Joe Davis.

Think Team

> "The leaders who work most effectively, it seems to me, never say 'I.' And that's not because they have trained themselves not to say 'I.' They don't think 'I.' They think 'we'; they think 'team.' They understand their job to be to make the team function. They accept responsibility and don't sidestep it, but 'we' gets the credit… This is what creates trust, what enables you to get the task done."
>
> —*Peter F. Drucker*

Trader Joe's is not your typical grocery store—not for its customers or its crew members, the moniker used for their store employees. Crew members report to the "first mate" (assistant store manager), who, in turn, reports to the "captain" (store manager). New crew members are selected, in part, for their enthusiasm and energy. As part of the on-boarding process, Trader Joe's gives crew members training that includes skills in communication, teamwork, leadership, and product knowledge.

Trader Joe's solidifies a strong sense of community by rotating enthusiastic crew members through different jobs within the store: from cashier, to stocker, to customer service. This builds compassion among crew members and eliminates boundaries that can form between different roles. They also encourage a fun and casual South Seas atmosphere through crew members wearing Hawaiian shirts, as well as banners located throughout the store, that convey the theme. Friendships are easy to come by at the store, and employees often like to socialize outside of work. On a regular basis, the "first mate" holds voluntary meetings after closing to taste and talk about the wine and food products sold in the store. Crew members show up to learn and share their knowledge, along with a few laughs.

Team Organization

"A business of trying to do new things doesn't lend itself to regimentation."

—*Livio D. Desimone*

Fireman's Fund Insurance Company's Personal Coverage Insurance Division in Novato, California, divided its employees into natural work units organized around its customers. The number of management levels was cut, and more individuals were assigned whole jobs instead of fragmented work tasks. As a result, employees felt they had a real stake in making customers happy, efficiency increased by 35 to 40 percent, systems investments declined by $5 million a year, and endorsement turnaround was cut from twenty-one *days* to twenty-four to forty-eight *hours*.

Facebook forms teams around people's passions. From the moment a new hire arrives, he or she is instructed to "take a look around, figure out what the problems or opportunities are, and help bridge them." Employees are encouraged to form teams around projects they're passionate about because Facebook's leaders understand that great work comes from doing what you love. Regardless of a person's level in the organization, staff members can turn ideas into products. "Pixels talk," said Joey Flynn, one of the designers of the Facebook timeline, in an article in *Entrepreneur* magazine. "You can do anything here if you can prove it."

Customer Focus

> "Spend a lot of time talking to customers face-to-face. You'd be amazed how many companies don't listen to their customers."
>
> —*Ross Perot*

At Good Eggs, a San Francisco–based digital marketplace where shoppers connect with independent, local food producers in and around their metro area, every customer order for fruits and vegetables is picked from the freshest produce currently available in the field. To reinforce the company's core value of having each team member fully understand all aspects of the business, each new hire initially works in all departments of the company, including direct contact with farmers and customers. Listening to concerns directly gives employees firsthand knowledge of what's really important to customers.

Your most unhappy customers are your

GREATEST
SOURCE OF
LEARNING.

—Bill Gates

Empower Employees

"An empowered organization is one in which individuals have the knowledge, skill, desire, and opportunity to personally succeed in a way that leads to collective organizational success."

—*Stephen R. Covey*

3M (formerly known as the Minnesota Mining and Manufacturing Company), a diversified manufacturer with more than $30 billion in annual sales, has long had a reputation for empowering employees. To spur innovation, for example, 3M encourages members of its technical and engineering staff to spend 15 percent of their work time pursuing projects of their own choosing. At Google, up to 20 percent of each employee's time can be spent on projects of his or her choosing.

Pixar's delightful and wildly successful family films are created by a team of down-to-earth artists who believe in themselves. This is the secret of Pixar's success. They build this culture by avoiding what they call "No, but…" This means that when someone suggests an idea, others should respond with "Yes, and…," not "No, but…" This philosophy was brought to Pixar by the late Joe Ranft, their head of storytelling for many years. It derives from the concept that, as they say on campus, "Every idea is a good idea." Pixar strives to create the most trusting environment possible for their employees, where people follow their own vision and are allowed to make mistakes.

Too often, decisions move up the management chain to people who have the least amount of knowledge to make the best decision. Big decisions shouldn't always be made by management. Empower employees to make decisions that apply to their own groups and roles. In addition to speeding up decisions and helping shape current team members into future managers, this will also instill a sense of ownership throughout your team. At W. L. Gore & Associates, Inc., makers of GORE-TEX and other products, employees are encouraged to use a boating analogy— "above or below the waterline"—in making decisions. If a boat gets a hole above the waterline, it isn't at risk of sinking; if the hole is below the waterline, it is in immediate danger. Likewise, employees are charged with considering the risk of all decisions they make; if the risk is great, they are asked to get broader assurances that it is the best decision prior to proceeding.

Texas Commerce Bank in Houston, Texas, used a slow period in the market as an opportunity to empower employees to improve both their internal processes and customer service. Focus groups were formed to identify and fix systemic problems that frustrated both employees and customers. For example, if tellers spent thirty seconds on one step in a process they had to do one hundred times per day, it added up to a significant cost. The bank gave the focus groups permission to tackle these problems and find solutions. At the onset, the company estimated that the teams' efforts would net a total savings of $50 million, but, in fact, the resulting cost savings were double that amount.

Live Your Values

"It's not hard to make decisions when you know what your values are."

—*Roy E. Disney*

Montefiore Nursing Home in Beachwood, Ohio, a nonprofit facility, started a Keys to Our Commitment program in which teams promise to uphold certain values, such as helping one another, serving patient needs, or being helpful to relatives. Workers are challenged to never say "I don't know." Staff members who embody a value are awarded paper keys by fellow staffers. They can then trade them for pins, from bronze to gold. For instance, ten paper keys equal one bronze pin. The program has helped employees work more cooperatively, share information with management, and feel more supported. Turnover has been cut in half.

We talk a lot about
HOPE, HELPING,
and **TEAMWORK.**

Our whole message is that we are more powerful **TOGETHER.**

—*Victoria Osteen*

How Great Teams Work

"A successful team is a group of many
hands but of one mind."

—*Bill Bet*

One manager I interviewed at what was formerly
BankBoston had sixty-five direct reports and inter-
acted with each of them every day. When asked, "How
do you get your job done if you spend so much time
interacting with employees," she replied, "Spending
time with employees is my job."

To promote teamwork, employees at L. Norman
Howe & Associates in Pasadena, California, make lists
of their tasks or projects every Monday morning. The
lists are shared with supervisors and read out loud to

employees at a one-hour staff lunch. Coworkers often suggest new ways to approach tasks or offer to help one another out.

Reinforcement doesn't have to come only after the end goal has been met. Make a point of checking in with workers, both individually and with the entire group, making positive comments about their collaborative efforts and offering any help they may need. Don't take over the decision-making for them, and don't apply pressure to meet artificial deadlines. It's a very powerful message to trust a group to solve a problem on its own.

Improve the Environment

"Men and women want to do a good job, a creative job, and if they are provided the proper environment, they will do so."

—Bill Hewlett

To foster innovation, teamwork, and collaboration, Google Ventures uses the walls of a dedicated space they call their war room as a canvas for shared note-taking and as long-term storage space for projects in progress. When working on a project, employees at Google Ventures capture every decision using whiteboards, Post-it Notes, or writing on glass windows. The more they put on the walls, the more shared understanding they build. *Fast Company* listed Google Venture's recommendations for creating a great war room:

- LOTS OF SURFACE AREA. To accommodate all the information you want to capture, you need a lot of space, including windows, empty walls, and as many whiteboards as you can fit.
- DEDICATED TO PROJECTS *(not meetings)*. Don't turn your war room into just another conference room. For best results, remove it from the company's room-scheduling calendar.
- FLEXIBLE FURNITURE. Sometimes you will want chairs and open space to invite discussion. Other times, you will want desks for writing or drawing. The ideal war room has furniture that's lightweight or on wheels, so it's easy to move.

Give Initiative Free Reign

"They always say time changes things, but you actually have to change them yourself."

—*Andy Warhol*

One hot summer day, Dina Campion, a Starbucks district manager, threw ice in a coffee drink and blended it. She tried it, liked it, started making it for coworkers, and then started selling the cold coffee drink to customers. She received an edict from the corporate office saying staff couldn't just start selling items randomly and must stop. Fortunately, Dina believed in the idea enough to wait until the end of the month to be able to report a full month's sales results. She subsequently received a call from Howard

Schultz, Starbucks CEO, thanking her for ignoring the edict she had received and sticking with an idea she believed in. Dina had created the Frappuccino, which became a $50 million dollar product line the first year it rolled out.

One of 3M's employees, Art Fry, sang in a choir at the Cathedral of St. Paul and used index cards in his hymnal to mark the next hymn to sing. Unfortunately, the index cards would often fall out. It seemed to Art that 3M could figure out how to put a low-grade adhesive on a piece of paper so it would stick to another piece of paper. The research department at 3M told him it would never work because it would be very difficult to get consistency in a low-grade adhesive. Art's response: "That's great news, because it means that when we figure out how to do it, it will be hard for our competition to duplicate." He wasn't dissuaded and took his idea to the marketing department which tested the product in seven different markets and concluded the product was a bomb. Art said they tested it wrong, so he and a buddy walked the streets of St. Paul, Minnesota, and gave out free samples to small businesses (the first time in the history of 3M free samples had been used!). He came back a week later, and 90 percent of the businesses wanted to order more. After that, Art started distributing "the yellow pads of paper" to administrative assistants within 3M until overwhelming popularity led it to become an official new product. In its first year, Post-it Notes became a $300 million product line.

Deal with Change

> "A corporation is a living organism; it has to continue to shed its skin. Methods have to change. Focus has to change. Values have to change. The sum total of those changes is transformation."
>
> —*Andrew Grove*

"Be vulnerable with your staff," said Paul Spiegelman, founder of BerylHealth, a call-center business in Bedford, Texas. "Tell them you want to change things, then ask, 'How do we do this together?' We can't guess what's important to employees. We have to give them ways to communicate with us. And we have to get out of our comfort zone as leaders. The more personal you can be in any situation, while being professional, that's the way to do it."

Make Meetings Matter

"Meetings, clearly, can take place anywhere, and wouldn't it be nice to see your coworkers lounging on the grass with their shoes off?"

—*Tom Hodgkinson*

Owens Corning in Toledo, Ohio, uses *open space* meetings to open communication and improve productivity among team members. Open space meetings, pioneered by Anglican priest and management consultant Harrison Owen, have no agenda, planned sessions, or scheduled speakers. Participants sit in a circle, and anyone who feels passionate about a topic and is willing to lead a breakout session can step into the center of the circle and announce his name and topic. The topic is written on a chart and posted on the wall. After all topics are listed, everyone participates in as many breakout groups as they desire.

Daily, ten-minute meetings make virtual teams successful. ClientSuccess, a startup company based in Lehi, Utah, uses such meetings on Skype to manage their virtual teams. All team members are required to attend these morning meetings, which set the context for the coming day's work. The ten-minute duration keeps discussion brief but relevant. This time is not used for problem-solving; any issues raised are taken offline and dealt with by the relevant group after the meeting. At the meeting, each team member briefly discusses:

What did I do yesterday?

What will I do today?

Are there any impediments in my way?

Using this approach, the team gains an excellent understanding of what work has been done, what work remains, and what commitments team members must make to accomplish their goals.

Another meeting format that helps to keep the meeting focused and brief is to have a standing meeting. When people aren't so comfortable that their minds can drift, the objectives of the meeting can be achieved more quickly. To keep people focused on the speaker, have a simple rule that "participants can only speak if they are granted permission to speak." In his department meetings, this author once used a coconut that was passed from speaker to speaker to show who "had the floor."

Trust One Another

"The greater the loyalty of a group toward the group, the greater is the motivation among the members to achieve the goals of the group, and the greater the probability that the group will achieve its goals."

—*Rensis Likert*

Manufacturing company W. L. Gore & Associates, Inc., in Newark, Delaware, puts employees through a rigorous hiring process to be sure everyone who's hired fits its unique culture. In this company of more than ten thousand employees, no more than two hundred are in any one facility so employees can get to know one another; there are no titles, no special offices, no perks, just the ability—and the assumption—that anyone can talk to anyone else about any problem that needs to be solved. Leaders emerge in groups on the basis of trust others have in their judgment. With a smaller number of employees in one location, employees can talk directly to one another and work together, but the entire team is rewarded for successful completion of a project.

Problem Solving

"Problems can become opportunities when the right people come together."

—*Robert South*

At the Tennant Company in Minneapolis, Minnesota, engineers devised a $100,000 system to streamline a particular welding operation. When management determined that the system was too expensive, a small group of welders tackled the problem, devising an overhead monorail system out of I-beams from a local junkyard for less than $2,000. The system saved more than $29,000 in time and storage space, and the team of welders was energized by taking the initiative to solve the problem.

Share Knowledge

"Knowledge is power."

—Francis Bacon

Invest in an online knowledge-sharing platform. Access to knowledge—from other people and materials—inspires employees to work collaboratively and build teams. David Ogilvy, the late founder of advertising company Ogilvy & Mather, placed enormous emphasis on sharing knowledge within the company. To harvest valuable knowledge resting in people's heads and hard drives, Ogilvy invested in an internal IT-based community he called Truffles. As a gourmet, Ogilvy appreciated the rich taste of a truffle and believed that "people should search for knowledge with as much energy and enthusiasm as a pig searches for truffles in the oak forests of France."

As a database of company knowledge, Truffles allowed access to shared projects and provided an opportunity for employees to contribute ideas and insights through forums created for the hundreds of communities of interest that sprang up in the firm.

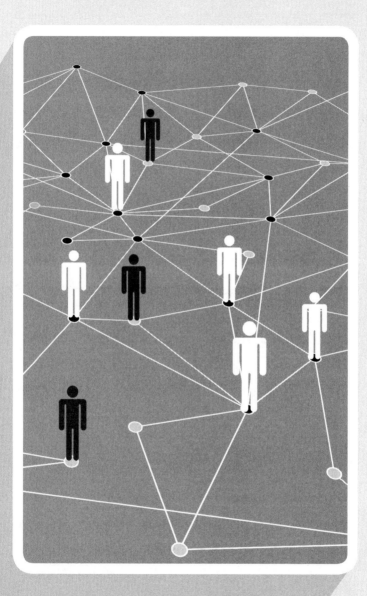

Promote Suggestions

"Many ideas grow better when transplanted into another mind than the one where they sprang up."

—*Oliver Wendell Holmes*

Over the last thirty years, Southwest Airlines has been the most profitable airline in America in part because all employees' ideas count. As an example, one of the most profitable ideas for the airline in the last decade came from an hourly baggage handler who suggested that some passengers wanted to board the plane first to select their desired seats so why not charge a little more for that privilege? Southwest tried his idea, and now, with Business Select, passengers can pay a little extra, board early, and get the seat selection they want.

Break Out
of the Mold

"When patterns are broken, new worlds emerge."
—*Tuli Kupferberg*

Huan Ho, cofounder of Rallyteam, an engagement and social media platform that allows employees to collaborate using a suite of social productivity tools in a single, unified platform, uses Evolution Fridays to constantly improve. Every second Friday, employees meet as a team to discuss what they can do to improve their teams or the company, looking for ways to break out of the mold and work on initiatives that evolve their systems, processes, and/or team. The only rule: it cannot be operational work and employees must have fun doing it!

At the meetings, team members take turns facilitating one of the sessions below:

- ROUND TABLE: Fifteen minutes to discuss evolution projects/goals, hold one another accountable, share ideas, and provide feedback.
- LESSONS LEARNED: Fifteen minutes to share lessons learned over the previous two weeks. Sometimes team members do a more formal training session or bring in guest speakers from other teams.
- LEADERS JOURNEY: Fifteen minutes of discussion on how team members can become better leaders, including examples of good leadership and reading/discussing articles on leadership.
- CHALLENGE/DEBATE: Fifteen minutes to complete a team challenge or debate. Often, topics were unrelated to work but helped to develop team communication/collaboration skills.

After the session, team members have the rest of the afternoon to work on evolution projects, which range from developing new forecasting models to organizing the next volunteer event. Huan Ho implemented Evolution Fridays with his team years ago and employees love it! Apart from building a stronger team, Rallyteam has directly improved their systems and processes as a result of Evolution Fridays.

We keep **MOVING FORWARD, OPENING NEW DOORS,** and **DOING NEW THINGS** because we're curious, and curiosity keeps leading us down new paths.

Encourage Team Participation

"Think like a wise man but communicate in the language of the people."

—*William Butler Yeats*

Ben & Jerry's, the ice cream company, distributes grants to departments at its corporate headquarters in South Burlington, Vermont, that come up with creative suggestions for the workplace. Groups can use the grants to purchase what they want for their team, such as popcorn makers or hot chocolate machines.

Many work teams start out with great intentions and then slowly lose momentum. How can team leaders and team members pump life back into a tired team? Be creative. Use Continuous Positive

Reinforcement (CPR) to put teams back on track and keep them excited about their work. Positive reinforcement is anything that makes a team or team member feel good. The positive reinforcement could be in the form of recognition, special opportunities, awards, freedoms, achievement—anything that meets the team's or a team member's needs.

Recognize Great Work

"A group becomes a team when each member is sure enough of himself and his contribution to praise the skills of the others."

—Norman Shidle

The silliest things can have a profound impact. At Hewlett-Packard, when a software engineer found a software bug, his manager, knowing the importance of timely recognition, wanted to capture the moment and handed him a banana from his own lunch, telling him "Great job!" Over time, the Golden Banana Award has become HP's most prestigious award, complete with a plaque and a banana lapel pin. Receiving the

Golden Banana Award puts employees in an elite performers' club.

At the Good Samaritan, a nursing home in West Union, Iowa, cross-functional teams have been created for every shift, consisting of a registered nurse, a dietitian, and patient care aides for each wing. Teams are recognized at quarterly get togethers for the number of compliments they receive from patients and their relatives or from administrators. Comment cards are read aloud and posted on the central bulletin board, and administrators bring baked goods or flowers from their own gardens to recognize the team with the most favorable comments that quarter.

Recognize the Team

"If anything goes bad, I did it. If anything goes semi-good, we did it. If anything goes really good, then you did it. That's all it takes to get people to win football games for you."

—*Paul "Bear" Bryant*

The Wildwood Management Group, a homeowners' association management company based in San Antonio, Texas, uses the Bell Ringer Award to celebrate successes as a team and to systematically build a positive work culture. When employees have good news to share, such as a positive letter received from a homeowner, they send an email to their leader about the good news. After seeing the email, the leader rings a bell on his or her desk and forwards the message to everyone in the office, prompting them to stop and read the good news while ringing their own bell used just for this purpose. Positive comments from clients are posted on Facebook and also scrolled on a plasma screen in the office lobby.

"Any disgruntled homeowner who comes in to make a complaint sees all the accolades our team has received from other homeowners," said Yvonne Weber, who manages the firm. "It causes people to pause and think, 'Wow, these are some great people!'"

A manager at ESPN starts each staff meeting by asking the group to name five things that are going well. Sometimes this is easy and they quickly move on. Sometimes they have to work at it because things are not going that well, but they don't proceed to the meeting's agenda until they can do this, reinforcing their confidence in their ability to take on and resolve whatever issues are needed. Similarly, at Bank of

COMPANIES DON'T SUCCEED, PEOPLE DO!

America, all meetings of any size are started with some type of recognition to thank and acknowledge people for achievements they have had.

Reward Your Team

"The reward of a work is to have produced it;
the reward of effort is to have grown by it."

—*Antonin Sertillanges*

At Atlanta, Georgia–based Delta Airlines, employees fill out a team recognition card to give to teams they feel have gone "above and beyond." Cards are entered in a drawing, with $500 donated to a charity or civic organization of the team's choice.

Simpler ideas are easier to implement, and they work well. At the Dow Chemical Company, they host ice-cream socials to celebrate successes, served by managers and executives of the firm. At San Bruno, California–based Gap, Inc., a manager gave out spa gift certificates after a team worked frantically to meet a deadline. It provided a much-appreciated way for employees to relax.

SIMPLER
ideas are easier to

implement, and
they work well.

About the Author

Dr. Bob Nelson is considered one of the leading authorities on employee recognition, motivation, and engagement. He is president of Nelson Motivation, Inc., in San Diego, California, a management training and consulting company that specializes in helping organizations improve their management practices, programs, and systems. He serves as an executive strategist for human resources issues and has worked with 80 percent of the Fortune 500. He previously worked closely with Dr. Ken Blanchard, coauthor of *The One Minute Manager*, for ten years and is currently a personal coach for Dr. Marshall Goldsmith, the top-ranked executive coach in the world.

Dr. Bob has sold four million books on management and motivation, including *1501 Ways to Reward Employees*, which recently went into its sixty-second printing, *The 1001 Rewards & Recognition Fieldbook: The Complete Guide* (with Dean Spitzer), *1001 Ways to Energize Employees*, *1001 Ways to Take Initiative at Work*, *Ubuntu!* (with Stephen Lundin), and *The Management Bible* (with Peter Economy), among others. He received an MBA in organizational behavior from the University of California–Berkeley and earned his PhD in management with the late, great Dr. Peter Drucker, the father of modern management, at the Peter F. Drucker Graduate Management School at Claremont Graduate University in Los Angeles. He teaches for the MBA program at the Rady School of Management at the University of California–San Diego.

COMPANIES DON'T SUCCEED, PEOPLE DO!

Dr. Bob is available to present for companies, conferences, and associations. For more information, please contact him directly at bob@drbobnelson.com or visit his website at www.drbobnelson.com.